'Night, Zoo

Library of Congress Cataloging-in-Publication Data

Bernal, Richard.
'Night, zoo / written and illustrated by Richard Bernal.
p.   cm.
''A Calico book.''
Summary: At bedtime bear cubs snuggle up against their mother,
a drowsy woodchuck curls up in its burrow, and a
penguin family settles down for a good night's sleep.
ISBN 0-8092-4396-2 : $11.95
1. Animals—Juvenile poetry.   2. Night—Juvenile poetry.
3. Children's poetry, American.   [1. Animals—Poetry.   2. Bedtime—
Poetry.   3. American poetry.]   I. Title.   II. Title: Goodnight,
zoo.   III. Title: Good night, zoo.
PS3552.E72575N54   1989
811'.54—dc19   88-8532
                                                                                    CIP
                                                                                    AC

Published by Contemporary Books, Inc.
180 North Michigan Avenue, Chicago, Illinois 60601
Manufactured in the United States of America
International Standard Book Number: 0-8092-4396-2

Published simultaneously in Canada by Beaverbooks, Ltd.
195 Allstate Parkway, Valleywood Business Park
Markham, Ontario L3R 4T8 Canada

'Night, Zoo

Written and Illustrated by

RICHARD BERNAL

A CALICO BOOK

Published by Contemporary Books, Inc.
CHICAGO • NEW YORK

'Night, Chimpanzees

'Night, Gazelles

'Night, Woodchuck

'Night, Herons

'Night, Penguins

'Night, Soft-Shelled Turtles

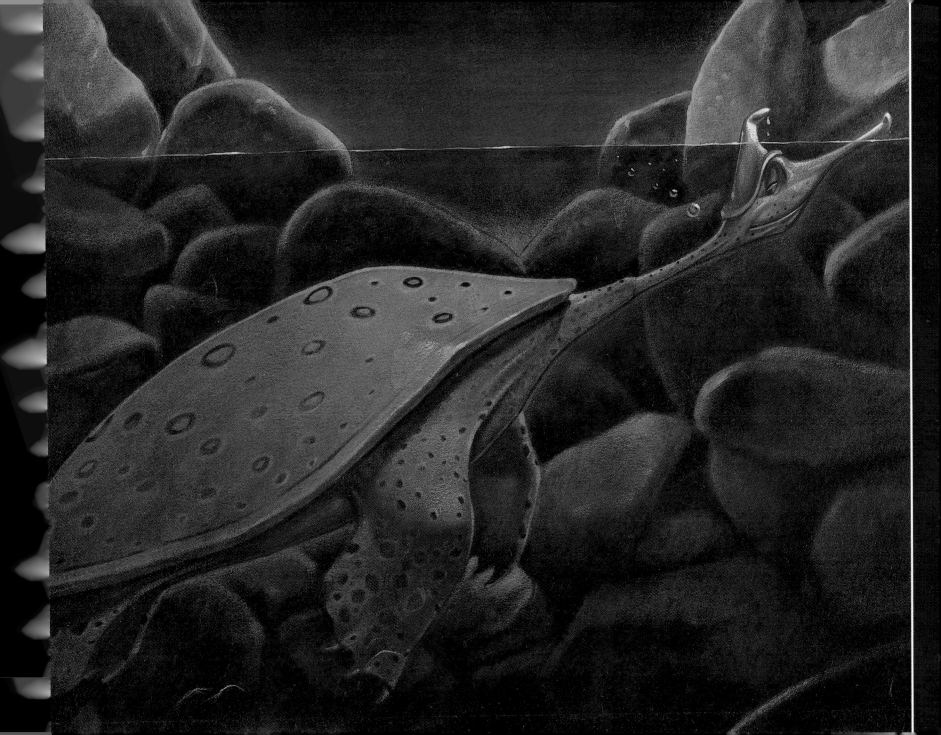

'Night, Bears

'Night, Leopards

'Night, Zoo

DATE DUE
